CW00621327

Mothers

The Light of Their Children's World

Dr Agnes Odejide

A Odejide

Jesus Joy Publishing

First Published and printed in Great Britain in 2011 by
Jesus Joy Publishing a division of Eklegein Ltd

© Dr Agnes Odejide

Cover Design: Ola-Tokunbo Aworinde and Pelumi Aworinde
Charisma Creations (Nigeria) Limited
www.charismacreations.biz

ISBN 978-1-90797-107-5

Jesus Joy Publishing

A division of Eklegein Ltd

www.jesusjoypublishing.co.uk

20181011

Dedication

This book is dedicated to the memories of my mother, my mother-in-law, my younger sister, Folake, and to all the other wonderful women in my life as well as to all my biological and spiritual daughters.

May you be a true light in your children's world.

Amen.

Foreword

The sacredness, sanctity and special significance of the mother are clearly depicted in the fact that, whilst at creation God made man first and then woman, He decided the incarnation would be through Mary.

Biologically, both male and female have their contributory roles in reproduction; but after fertilisation has occurred within the female, her entire physiology and psychology begin the process of adaptation towards the development of the growing baby. All her habits like eating, drinking and working could affect the embryo. She is not just a container as corresponding changes take place as the baby develops within her body! In essence therefore, motherhood is a sacrifice and a risk that can be fatal.

Spiritually, maternal influence is also of utmost importance. For example Timothy was commended by Paul when he remarked that

Timothy's faith was a follow-on of his mother Eunice and grandmother Lois. [2 Timothy 1:5]

This book on Mothers contains a lot of worthy accounts of motherly affection, diligence and dedication of three mothers who impacted positively on their children's lives. Written from personal experiences without inhibition or exaggeration of what a true mother can be under the guidance of God, it is a worthy manual for mothers, fathers, would-be mothers and indeed for all.

The book also highlights for all, the supportive role of the father. Usually mothers are the 'Ministers of Home Affairs' in the family 'cabinet', but they tend to take on more ministries to assist the father whose encompassing role is also aptly described in the book. Thus, the father's section blended easily with the other sections because as Christians, father and mother are inextricably bound as one. The father emphasises prayers thereby ensuring that prayer is the 'key' to the day and the 'lock' of the night. Throughout the day, the chain of prayer needs to be externalised in prayerful work.

Finally, I would also commend with very great delight the practical way the book was put together. One senses the unity of the Spirit; sights the unison and cohesion in a godly family where the love of God has been visibly and audibly at work for the past 40 years! Our God is faithful.

As you read, pray and apply. May your own home be a foretaste of eternity with the Lord. Happy and blessed reading.

Dr. Ebenezer Dupe Akinluyi

(Fellow of the Royal College of Obstetricians and Gynaecologists)

Contents

Introduction

By today's social norms, my mother would be regarded as a 'single parent'. She had been married to Mr. Joseph Falajiki (of blessed memory) - the father of my older sister, Mrs Esther Oloruntola Ajayi, my older brother, Engineer Samuel Kolawole Falajiki and my younger sister, Mrs Julianah Folake Aworinde (of blessed memory). However, the circumstances surrounding my birth, which I did not know about until I was about the age of 13, were such that she was forced out of her matrimonial home where there were three other wives.

When my mother was expecting me, she lived first with her uncle and later moved to a spiritual home where I was delivered. From there, she moved to one of her aunties' house where she lived with me for several years before she moved back to her husband.

She never lived with my father! Thus, I was

raised neither in a typical polygamous family nor a nuclear Christian family, as my children have enjoyed. Nevertheless, today I have no regrets about my early childhood for I believe that God allowed the circumstances surrounding my birth to show forth the power of His Love and Grace.

I am not ashamed to tell the story of my birth for I believe that my birth was not an accident - it was planned by God who states

> *"'For I know the **plans** I have for **you**'*
> *declares the LORD, 'plans to **prosper you***
> *and not to harm you, plans to give you*
> ***hope** and a future.'"*

[Jeremiah 29:11 emphasis added]

This Bible verse is so true and has been so relevant to me. Personally, I can say like Abraham Lincoln that *"All that I am and ever hope to be I owe to my angel Mother"*[1]

Why This Book On Mothers?

A story is told of a child in Sunday School who

forgot his memory verse while on the stage. Naturally, he looked towards his mother who was sitting in the front row to cheer him on. His mother, realising the predicament of her son (as mothers usually do) whispered *"I am the Light of the World."* [John 8:12] The three-year-old boy, a perfect lip reader then proudly and confidently said *"my mother is the light of the world!"*

When I read this story, my mind went back to my own mother. I can confidently say that my mother (of blessed memory) was 'the light of my world.' I started wondering if my grown-up children would think of me as a light in their world. I wonder how many mothers are thought of as 'the light of their children's world.'

What does my husband think of his mother, that is, my second mother? What about my late younger sister? Do her children think of her as a light in their world even though that light seems to have been prematurely extinguished? As mothers or mothers-to-be, what are the guidelines to follow which make us a light in our children's world? What is the role of fathers or fathers-to-be in making 'the light' (mothers) shine all the more? These and other questions of Christian family life are addressed in this book.

The book is in five chapters:

Chapter one is my testimony about my mother while,

Chapter two is my husband's testimony about his mother (my second mother).

Chapter three is about another mother that I can confidently confirm as 'the light of her children's world' - my late younger sister, Folake Aworinde.

Chapter four explains the role of the father in making the mother's light shine more brightly, not only in their children's world but also in the 'family' as a whole. Without the love and encouragement of the father, 'the light' can only shine dimly.

The final chapter challenges women to strive to be like the virtuous woman described in Proverbs 31 and gives some practical guidelines to mothers as to how to be 'the light of their children's world.'

The Postscript contains my first daughter's comments, herself a mother of two, about the book.

Chapter One

My Childhood Days

"A little girl, asked where her home was, replied, 'where mother is.'" [2]

My childhood days are very aptly depicted by the little girl's answer above. My remembrance of a home was a communal home in the compound of the prophet Baba Aladura - 'the daddy of prayers'. My mother was my first love; there was nobody else. I can truthfully say that all I am I owe to my mother. I attribute all my success in life to the spiritual, moral and physical education I received from her.

There were other families, mostly women and their children, in the prophet's compound where I lived with my mother. I must have been about five or six years of age at the time. I do not have any recollection of where we were living before then.

Why a 'Spiritual' Home?

In the late 1930s, a new wave of spiritual revival had come to Ikere-Ekiti, my mother's home town. Notable among such movements was the Christ Apostolic Church (CAC) founded by Apostle Ayo Babalola. My mother, like many others, moved from the Anglican Denomination to join the CAC.

Prominent in the CAC doctrine was the emphasis on powerful prayers, fasting, speaking in tongues, and seeing visions. Independent prophets must have emerged as offshoots of the CAC doctrine. Many who perceived that they needed protection from their 'enemies', moved to live in the compounds of prophets where there would be powerful prayers and fasting at times for 24 hours a day and seven days a week, depending on the seriousness of the perceived danger facing the residents.

My first recollection of my mother was of a hardworking, loving and prayerful woman. She would go for days in prayer and fasting to counteract any vision of pending danger to me - her 'baby Sayo'. As far as I can remember, I was not suffering from any illness but it seemed I needed to be 'protected' especially from those who would want to kill me (with juju or witchcraft) to spite my mother. My two older siblings were not living with us in the prophet's compound.

As far as I can remember, my mother did not tell me anything about my father. I suppose I was too young and too protected to feel the need for a father. And in any case, there were other children living with their mothers in the same compound whose fathers were not visiting. It was Baba Aladura whom all of us, young and old, looked up to as our father.

The next place I remember my mother and I living was with her aunty in another part of the town. It was while we were living there that I began to notice a man visiting us regularly. I later came to regard this man as 'my father'. He renamed me - I was now to be called 'Omowumi' not Feyisayo. I was very proud of my new name and I gladly announced to everyone that my name was now 'Omowumi' meaning 'I love children'. I would refuse to answer anyone who called me by my former name Feyisayo meaning 'take this as joy!' I was later to know the real interpretation and the background stories and reasons behind these names. As young as I was at that time, some questions were already bothering me - .

Why were my mother and I not living with 'my father'? Where did he live? Why did we not attend church together? Why were my other siblings not living with us?

I was not to know the answers to these questions until much later.

My Spiritual Upbringing

My spiritual foundation is aptly described in Proverbs 22 which says *"Train up a child in the way he should go and when he is old, he will not depart from it. "* [Proverbs 22:6] I learnt through my mother how to fast and pray at a very early age. My mother would never miss church. Naturally, I went along and I was very active at the Sunday school.

I loved Bible memory verses and my favourite was Psalm 23 which I knew word for word:

"The Lord is my Shepherd. I shall not be in want.
He makes me lie down in green pastures,
He leads me beside quiet waters,
He restores my soul.

He guides me in paths of righteousness for his name's sake.
Even though I walk through the valley of the shadow of death,
I will fear no evil, for you are with me;
Your rod and your staff, they comfort me.

You prepare a table before me in the presence of my enemies.
You anoint my head with oil;
My cup overflows.

Surely goodness and love will follow me all the days of my life, And I will dwell in the house of the Lord forever."

My Sunday School teacher liked me and it was he who first discovered my potential for quick assimilation and retention of all I was taught. He was convinced very early that I was a candidate for proper schooling. I was already about eight years old at this time. One day the Sunday School teacher told me that he had told my mother that I should be sent to school. He then advised me to tell her that I would like to go to school.

So when I got home, I told my mother that I would like to go to school. She told me that 'my father' would have to approve. She then advised me that I should tell 'my father', with tears if need be, that I would like to go to school and she would then support my request. What a wise counsel!

So it was, that whenever 'my father' visited, I would start to pester him by reciting all that I had learnt in Sunday School to show him how clever I was, and by shedding tears occasionally to reinforce my desire to go to school! After weeks of such pestering, the poor man reluctantly gave in on the condition that my mother would be the one responsible for the school fees and all that schooling would entail. Education, even at the primary school level, was not free at that time.

My mother, 'the light of my world', happily agreed to take up the responsibility. She told me in later years that she had made up her mind much earlier that *"this child must go to school."* I often wonder today where I would be if my mother did not take up the responsibility of my education at this crucial stage. If she did not, how would I have ever become what I am today? My Mother was truly 'the light of my world'; although an illiterate, she recognised the value of education and was prepared to make the necessary sacrifice to ensure I would receive a good education

Primary School Education

I started my primary education at St. Matthew's Apostolic Church Primary School, Ikere-Ekiti in January 1953 and finished in 1958 (a record time as I was given a double promotion one year). My mother was fully responsible for my primary education. It was not easy for her financially but she was determined. By the time I finished primary school, she was already thinking about how I would further my education.

Secondary School Education

Children from comfortable homes were able to pay for the Common Entrance Examination forms for secondary schools. My mother could not afford to pay for the form. So I had to apply for the Modern School entrance form which was much cheaper.[3] I passed the entrance examination easily so I was given admission to the Modern School. However, my mother was still struggling to gather the required deposit that would confirm my place in the Modern School when a divine intervention took place!

One day, my mother asked me to read a letter written to her by her sister living in Lagos.[4] It was not unusual for my mother to ask me to read letters to her (she could neither read nor write; the only books she could read in the Yoruba dialect were the Bible and the Hymn books). However, I was not in the least prepared for what I read in that letter. For in the letter, my aunty, Mrs Phoebean Fehintola Olagbaiye (of blessed memory) was encouraging my mother to send me to my 'real' father and that she should stop bearing the burden of my education alone. But who was my 'real' father?

The Revelations

I was about thirteen years of age when my mother made the following revelations to me:

- My biological father was Mr. Michael Bamigbola Bewaji who had come to teach at the CAC Primary school before I was born.

- My mother had had to separate from her husband Mr Falajiki (my current 'father') because of a secondary infertility of about 9 years!

- When I was a few months old, my father, Mr. Bewaji was transferred from Ikere.

- My mother would not abandon her two other children (my older sister, Oloruntola and my older brother, Kola).

- My mother, being an illiterate, could only communicate with my father for a few years.

- After a separation from her husband for about seven years, there were moves to reconcile them. This was when Mr. Falajiki my current 'father' started to visit us. Their coming together resulted into the birth of another child, my late younger sister, Mrs Julianah Folake Aworinde. So it was that of the four of us born by my mother, I was the only one from a different father; my two older siblings and my younger sister were of the same father Mr Falajiki. These were intriguing revelations indeed!

My mother told me that for about a year before the revelations Mr. Bewaji had been communicating with her through his cousin, Mr. Ezekiel Ajetumobi who had come to teach at CAC primary school. She told me that my father wanted me to come and live with him and that if I was happy to go, she would release me. Of course, this was a great sacrifice on her part, but she knew that releasing me at that time was the surest way for me to further my education. Thus, like Renita Weems[5], my mother was 'my bridge' – "When I needed to get across, she steadied herself long enough for me to run across safely."

My mother was indeed the light of my world! How would I have become what I am today if not for her? I was already in my early teens when I went to live with my biological father. If my mother had not financed my primary education, certainly I would not have had any formal education. I would probably have been married off to a local farmer or bricklayer and not to my darling husband of almost 40 years who is an internationally-recognised Obstetrician and Gynaecologist. Praise be to God! My mother continued to play constructive roles in my life until the Lord called her home in the year 2000:

My Marriage and Family

In my experience it is very true that very often *"only a Mother's faith can help us on life's way and inspire in us the confidence we need from day to day."*[6] My mother's love and faith were vividly manifest when I was faced with what I thought was a 'major' disappointment - a failed relationship. I remember how at the crucial time she taught me to fast and pray. I did and I thank God today that my mother's faith has helped me on life's way and has inspired in me the confidence that I need from day to day. Now as a mother, I have had opportunities to share 'joys' and 'tears' with my children. My marriage/family is what it is today because of my mother's wise counsel. During the first four years of my marriage, my husband was still a student. My mother was a pillar of support in prayers, kindness, cash and godly counsel. When my husband and I decided to set up the Living Hope Hospital, she shared our vision and was fully with us prayerfully and financially.

My Mother And My Children

My mother loved and took care of each of my children. She became 'the physiotherapist' when Temilolu broke his arm during a 'break dancing' practice. Her name is Fayoke for Olutomi, Opeyemi for Oluwaseun, and Oluwakemi for Oreofe. She loved our youngest child, Oluwadara, in a special way and named her Tolulope.

My Mother And My Husband

My mother loved and respected my husband and appreciated his wisdom and his dedication to the things of the Lord. Oh yes, my mother was 'the light of my world!' Even though my mother has gone to glory over ten years ago, I still 'carry her inside of me'; not in a negative and morbid way but because I also want to be seen and remembered by my children as a light in their lives, so help me God!

Chapter Two

My Second Mother

"Once blessed with a wonderful mother, I am twice blessed with my mother-in-law."

Author Unknown

A nother mother that I know who was truly 'the light of her children's world' was my mother-in-law, my second mother. My testimony about her is not the worldly testimony of mothers-in-law. She was my 'mother-in-love'. She accepted me fully as her own daughter and would often share her experiences in rearing her children in a typical polygamous family. She overcame the various challenges of secondary infertility, difficult childbirth experiences and the death of some of her children by showing selfless love to her husband, his other wives and their children. Like my first mother, my second mother was a 'Proverbs 31 Woman'. To buttress my observations about my 'second mother', I asked my husband, who was raised by this woman of many virtues, to write his testimony about his mother.

'My Mother Was A Light In Her Children's World'

Thomas Olatubosun Odejide

My mother was the first wife of my father – late Chief Daniel Abiona Odejide. He had three wives for different reasons not uncommon with the Yoruba culture some 100 years ago. She was born into a family that practiced traditional religion but became a Christian in her early years through the Baptist Mission at Iresi, Osun State, Nigeria.

Her father had promised his friend that she would be the wife of the his son. Her father died early and his friend's son left Iresi for another town. She grew up with her mother with whom she attended the Baptist Church in the rural town of Iresi. She learnt how to read some Yoruba through the Church Sunday School classes. She met and fell in love with my father through the Church.

A Devoted Lover To Her Husband

My maternal grandmother was very much against the relationship. My mother was expected to accept that she was already married on the basis of her father's promise before his death. She however was determined to marry the man whom she loved. She indeed got married to him and had a boy as their first child.

Barely under a year afterwards, the would-be Muslim husband returned to Iresi and went after her to claim her as his wife. According to her story, he was a powerful, native medicine man. My grandmother gave a good public cry knowing the danger into which her daughter had put her. Under pressure and fear, my mother and her baby were taken by the new man. My father, together with his people, appeared powerless to do anything about it. That was how a spiritual and legal local war started between my father and this new, powerful man who had taken his wife and son. Eventually my father won but not without paying a sad price as the baby died. Both my mother and my father had to leave Iresi in order to be far away from the man.

This story demonstrates the struggles of love marriages as opposed to a 'pre-arranged marriages'. This type of involuntary marriage was not uncommon during my mother's time. It is not quite like the 'arranged marriages' which are common in some cultures for example in India. Love always perseveres as the Bible says in 1 Corinthians 13.

My mother, Alice, suffered many things by accompanying my father to different parts of the Western Region of Nigeria in search of a means of livelihood. They finally settled at Oke-Awo village under Ile-Ife in Osun State as farmers. It was there that I was born.

A Lover And Tough Disciplinarian Of Children

My mother had a poor obstetric history with only

five of us surviving out of about 11 deliveries. I had a very handsome younger brother called Ezekiel who died about the age of six from smallpox. Both of us had it but I survived. I have three living sisters all doing well with their families. My only elder brother, Prof A. O. Odejide, died suddenly in January 2008 at the age of 68 years.

My mother suffered very much for us. I was close to her because my elder brother was born in 1939 while my immediate younger sister was born in 1952 and I was born 'kind of' in-between in 1945. I performed the tasks more usually undertaken by girls for my mother. She was a tough woman who tolerated no bad behaviour from us such as lying or stealing. She ensured that we attended the Church regularly and punctually. I was in the choir and used to look at her face for approval whenever we were rendering our 'special number'. Those were our foundational starting points in the Christian faith. She was very protective and defended us when we were in the right.

Her Love For My Wife

Her love and commitment to my wife was never in doubt. She was very protective of her. She was very close confidante to my wife in our early years of marriage. This had to change because of differences in generational value systems and levels of understanding on both our side and hers. She was always honest with us. I can remember my mother advising us to approach my father to make some medicine for us to ensure having a male child. Of course we nicely did not accept that advice. Throughout her life she saw us as one and respected our close bond. She was also a friend to my wife's mother whom I regarded as 'my mother', not just my mother-in-law. Glory to God.

A Woman With A Large Heart

"My mother had a slender, small body, but a large heart - a heart so large that everybody's joys found welcome in it, and hospitable accommodation."[7]

Mark Twain's description of his mother above was also true of my mother. My mother demonstrated her 'large-heartedness' in a typical polygamous home for many years. She accepted and treated my father's second wife as her sister. Much later when the third wife joined the family, she also was treated like a daughter (the third one is younger than her children). She accommodated all of them and showed them love practical ways. She was generous. She represented all the family children equally before our father. It must have been her faith in Jesus Christ that was on display.

An 'Educated' Woman

My mother was educated in her mind and vision. She was persistent in encouraging our father to send us to school. My father needed more hands on his farm and that meant men in particular. We were only two boys for my mother and the second wife had four boys by that time. Farming then was a promising economic business. With some encouragement from the Church, his first two boys (one each from the two mothers) were already at school. It was therefore not clear to me why my mother was encouraging me to trouble my father to send me to school.

I was already about ten years old and had grown to like farming because of the bonus of fresh vegetables and meat to eat daily. She had gone to solicit the help of other parents to talk to our father on the same issue. Thus, as Providence would have it and in answer to my mother's prayers and heart's desire, in 1956, five of us (three from my father and two of his nephew's children) were sent to school the same day!

What happened was that news had travelled to the village that the then progressive politician, Chief Obafemi Awolowo, Premier of the Western Region, had sent policemen to the villages to arrest parents who would not comply with his free primary education programme for the region. My mother spoke in support of both boys' and girls' education. I thank God that she lived long enough to see and enjoy the fruits of her labour.

A Counsellor And Leader

She was faithful to God in giving our father godly advice. On a few occasions she would even invite him to the Church so that he might hear hard truths and receive prayers. What a woman who feared God! She joined with my father (the village head) to run the affairs of the community. For more than the 20 years that he was the head, the community knew peace and progress. My mother was behind him all the way.

My father openly wished to be called to the home beyond before her but his wish was not granted as my mother was called home in 2001 at well over 80 years of age while papa died in 2005 at over 100 years.

A Grateful Woman

By the year 2000 she was diagnosed with advanced carcinoma of the stomach (her elder sister died of a similar illness). We gave her all the tender, loving, care we could up to year 2001. The Sunday that she died, I went to her at the Living Hope Hospital side room just before going to the Church. I sang a chorus which she sang with us. My cousin (the first child of her sister) was with her she also raised a chorus. Then I asked my mother to sing one of her own choice. Then she sang;

"Ope mi koito o, Ojojumo ni n o ma dupe; ope mi koito o, ojojumo ni n o ma yo"

which translates as

"my thanksgiving is not yet enough, everyday I will continue praising, my thanksgiving is not yet enough, everyday I will be rejoicing."

I then prayed a prayer of thanks to God and left for the Church. We returned from the Church about 1 p.m. and I went to see her only to be told that she had just taken her last breath. She died peacefully in the arms of my cousin. All glory to God for her life.

Chapter Three

'My Mom Lit Up My World'

My late sister, Mrs Folake Aworinde, was another mother who was a light in her children's world. This is why I have asked the eldest of her four children, Pelumi Aworinde to write this chapter. He testifies below how his mother was indeed 'the light of his world' and his siblings.

Pelumi reflects

In the Nigerian culture, when a child is born people can have one of two perspectives. One viewpoint regards this child with pity, believing that it has come to partake and contribute to the sorrow and struggling in the world around it.

The other perspective sees this child as a beacon of hope, a solution, a 'messiah' of its time, whose potential needs to be discovered, developed and deployed.

My mom, together with my dad, chose the latter paradigm when raising each of her four children. She chose relentlessly to pour illumination into the young minds of her brood during our formative years. As we developed and began to express our various interests, talents and fears, she kept pointing us in the right direction.

I remember growing up and watching my mother's attitude to the domestic maids who served us at different times. I remember how they would want to eat their meals in the kitchen sitting on low-level stools. My mother was not going to have any of that! She had an attitude whereby she treated each one of them as if they were her own children and therefore they were invited to eat their meals on the dining table like the rest of us. Thus began my understanding that every single person was meant to be treated with respect. She lived by example and therefore shone brighter and brighter to her 'perfect day'. As a result, we caught her fire and learnt to burn for Jesus. You see, my mom lit up my world.

Excerpt from 'Folake Live On' by Pelumi Aworinde[8]

"She was just the right kind of mother to me. She loved us all and taught us a lot of spiritual and ethical things. God used her to build me up to be a fine, young man. She did not fail to rebuke me when necessary — and she knew how to do it in love. She assisted me when I could not tell things to my dad although she always encouraged me to tell him myself.

"She was generous and objective. I will always remember and appreciate her submissiveness to my dad in quietness and gentleness of a spirit-filled woman. My mother was not necessarily a perfect person, but she was on her upward way to perfection radiating the fruit of the spirit."

'Momma's Faith'

In Mother's loving arms,
My head against her breast,
I felt a love so true
So true that I was blest.

She taught me as I grew
And nurtured me in truth,
Chastised me when I wronged
In the naiveté of youth.

She took the time to show
And teach me how to love
Not just the type down here
But love from up above.

If you look in Proverbs,
The very last chapter,
That's a good description
Of my mom's character.

She protected all her own
And also kept her own.
She prayed for all her own,
So truly loved her own.

She taught to trust in God,
He knows all that is best.
To put my faith in Him
And let Him do the rest.

When doctors gave no hope
And said her days would end.
Even deadly cancer,
Her faith it could not rend.

We prayed for her healing
And fasted for a change
But God did much better
Far beyond our range.

For ultimate healing,
He called her home to rest.
Rest from all her pains,
She had passed life's test.

Precious eyes closed in sleep,
Eternal sleep, sleep so deep.
Precious eyes closed in sleep,
Eternal sleep, sleep so deep.

We laid her now still body
Six feet under the earth.
She was no longer there,
She now knew new birth.

For those she left behind,
It was difficult to find,
The peace we all believed in.
To this we all seemed blind.

But God restored our hearts,
Gave us brand new comfort.
Comfort beyond all measure,
To heal us from all our hurt.

She had simply gone ahead
To our Master's bosom.
Joined the cloud of witnesses
And had fully blossomed.

Like in 1st Corinthians,
Chapter Number One,
We have now to comfort,
Those in need of some.

Truly those that believe
Truly they will receive
A true right to cleave
To Him who'll never leave.

Put your trust in Jesus,
He's true for evermore.
To be with Him forever,
Is worth the dying for!

With this deep in my mind.
My mom died not in vain.
The question I now ask you,
"Is your hope the same?"

In memory of My Mother, Mrs. Juliana Folake

Aworinde who went to be with Jesus on August 5th, 1996.

Chapter Four

Fathers Make Them Shine!

In the past 40 years, by the power of the Holy Spirit, I have tried to be a light in my secular work, our marriage and the church of God. Many brethren have testified positively about our marriage, spiritual and social activities as well as our worldly achievements, to the glory of God. I believe that 'mothers are the light of their children's world'. However, I also believe that fathers make that light shine brighter. This is why I have asked my husband to write the remainder of this chapter. How can fathers make the light shine more brightly? Here is his response.

A Sure Foundation

To make mothers shine, the marital foundation must be sure and steadfast. Our marital foundations must be laid on Christ Jesus, the corner-stone of every standing Christian home. When diverse storms like economic uncertainties, infertility, infidelity, poor health, external interferences against wealth and success, threaten a 'marital building', the guarantee that the house will stand rests upon its foundation. The author of marriage is God and His plan for marriage, between a man and a woman, is to last for the duration of their lives together on earth [Genesis 1:27, 2:24 & Matthew 19:4-6] His good purpose is that it should be like 'heaven on earth' for a man and his wife. When we agree with the One who cannot fail, then our marriage cannot fail to enjoy the blessings of the prayer of Jude

"To him who is able to keep you from falling and to present you before his glorious presence without fault and with great joy – to the only God our Saviour be glory, majesty, power and authority, through Jesus Christ our Lord, before all ages, now and forevermore. Amen"

[Jude 24-25]

By the grace that God has blessed us with, we have

resolved to stay together and fight the enemies of marriage and Christian homes under God's cover. I believe that it is the man's responsibility to take the lead in keeping the marital vow intact. The devil is the 'master enemy', not your spouse. Do not fight each other but join hands together to wage war against the devil.

Within the first five years of our marriage, there was a sharp disagreement which led to exchanges of hurtful words. The problem was caused by a relative who was staying with us at the time. At the height of the verbal conflict, my wife said that she would not care if that was the end of our marriage. At that point I saw that the devil was really at work and I called for a truce immediately. My wife also quickly woke up to what the devil was up to and that was how the problem ended peacefully. Since then we have never fallen into the temptation of allowing the idea of separation or divorce to cross our marital pathway. May the Lord bring healing to those who have suffered in regards to divorce. May the Lord bring them comfort and peace. He is a God who never gives up on any of His children and He will redeem and restore all that the enemy has stolen from you. Amen.

Husbands should make their wives shine by assuring them regularly that they will remain in love and in marriage with them *"until death do us part"*. Amen.

Fullness of Love

Love can be divided into four categories - Storge (family), Philia (friendship), Eros (romance), and Agape (unconditional love). All these types of love can and ought to be demonstrated in every Christian marriage. *"This is the Lord's doing and it is marvellous in our eyes."* [Psalm 118:23]

Adam and Eve were naked before each other and they were not ashamed. Biologically and emotionally God has created the man to initiate and sustain love. This is not just only on the honeymoon (Eros) days but for the rest of their lives. After a few years of living together and knowing each other, the love should graduate to 'Philia'. It is a kind of deep friendship that starts to develop between the two. It is a love that comes from intimacy and admiring new discoveries in each other.

Storge is manifested in the family especially when children as God's heritage, are added. It is the fondness through familiarity among family members.

Agape love is the highest and it is the *'God kind of love'* - totally unconditional. The characteristics of this real love are well spelt out in 1 Corinthians 13. It is a decision to love declared on the wedding day before a host of earthly and heavenly witnesses. When each declares, *"Yes I will"*, in answer to the officiating minister's question *"Will you marry this man/woman, for richer or poorer, in sickness or in health, until death parts you?"*, Heaven is behind that declaration and will cause there to be a fulfillment of the same for all those who remain married day by day in Jesus name. Amen.

Every man should work hard to help his wife and family to shine in these four areas of love. Giving spiritual leadership based on God's Word is the answer.

A Father Is A Man

God is looking for a man who will stand in the gap. It is very important to get God's leading before going into the business of marriage. It is a business where God expects from every man a good return of interest.

A Christian father is one who has achieved some degree of maturity in age, economic power or potential. He also needs a definite salvation faith in God through the Lord Jesus Christ with a commitment and steady fellowship with God and other believers. This man will be familiar with how God guides his children. He will marry according to the will and calling of God for his life.

This man will not abandon his responsibility to his wife and children. He will take care of them in every way. He will lift up his wife before his children. He will always praise and defend her. This is a sure way to make a woman shine as a mother. I give glory to God who is helping me to maintain this standard. There is still a lot of room for improvement for me. Thank you, Lord.

Starting Each Day

"Day by day, day by day, dear Lord
All these three things, I pray
To see thee more clearly,
Love thee more dearly
Follow thee more nearly,
Day by day..." [9]

The mood with which a day is started can have an impact on whether we make people around us shine or 'shrink.' Medically speaking, some of us do wake up with a tinge of a depressive or grumbling mood. The first person to be infected with that kind of gloomy mood is our spouse. You may hence start the day arguing over trivialities or gossiping about other people.

Fathers should accept the responsibility to prevent this happening as much as possible. Take the initiative to come into the presence of the Lord soon after waking up. *"In His presence there is joy and fullness of life."* [Psalm 16:11] Then bring your wife into fellowship with God confessing positively that *"this is the day that the Lord has made and we shall rejoice and be glad in it."* [Psalm 118:24] Prophesy good things into other people's lives starting with your children. Confess the word of God over whatever challenges you may face as a family.

Wives are often under greater emotional pressure, fathers must therefore always stand with their wives to encourage, defend and support them. This makes them shine.

The Power of Communication

The general rating of non-verbal communication as being higher and perhaps more important is very complex and debatable. I have no doubt that verbal communication is more potent positively and negatively. This is why the Word of God warns us about the use of our tongues. Words can heal or kill. The Bible makes it clear that *"from the abundance of the heart, the mouth speaks."* [Luke 6:45]

Words once spoken can hardly ever be taken back. Non-verbal or body language is not as dangerous, and if misread it can be denied. This is why I practice and admonish men and women to be very slow to speak just as the Bible says in James 1:19

Every man needs a lot of preventative prayers for wisdom and calm to know what appropriate communication tactics to apply in any provocative situation. Our aim should always be to help our wives to shine by making them happy. Pray for the grace and the enabling power to say "I am sorry" whether you feel like it or not. It brings healing to her and to you. Do not walk out of the house as some will advise. I consider this to be a very destructive non-verbal method of communication. You may go for a glass of water and calmly offer one to your wife just as you are saying *"I am sorry for this hurtful situation."* As the situation is calming down, give a gentle, loving hug and possibly a kiss as well! All these will work to calm anger.

Do not sleep with anger. It shortens one's life span! It makes God unhappy with you too. I am praying for more grace to be an agent of peace to my wife in verbal and non-verbal communication. Amen.

Finally, let me summarise the issues raised here in the words spoken to Paul Newman and Jeanne Woodward[10] on their wedding day. It was said that a happy marriage is:

- "not something that just happens. A good marriage must be created."

- "where the little things are the big things."

- "never being too old to hold hands."

- "remembering to say 'I love you' at least once a day. It is never going to sleep angry."

- " not taking the other for granted; the courtship should not end with the honeymoon, it should continue through all the years."

- "having a mutual sense of values and common objectives."

- "standing together facing the world. It is forming a circle of love that gathers in the whole family."

- "doing things for each other, not in the attitude of duty or sacrifice, but in the spirit of joy."

- "speaking words of appreciation and demonstrating gratitude in thoughtful ways."

- "not looking for perfection in each other."

- "cultivating flexibility, patience, understanding and a sense of humour."

- "having the capacity to forgive and forget."

- "giving each other an atmosphere in which each can grow."

- "finding room for the things of the spirit. It is a common search for the good and the beautiful."

- "is establishing a relationship in which the independence is equal, dependence is mutual and the obligation is reciprocal."

- "not only marrying the right partner, it is being the right partner."

So help us God. Amen.

Chapter Five

True Motherhood

"Sing, O barren woman, you who never bore a child; burst into song, shout for joy, you who were never in labour; because more are the children of the desolate woman than of her who has a husband", says the LORD.

[Isaiah 54:1]

Every woman is a potential mother. There are biological mothers, spiritual mothers and adopted mothers. In the sight of God, no woman shall be barren. The Bible confirms this in Isaiah 54 this is true motherhood.

Thus this chapter is relevant to all women, married or unmarried. After all, Mother Theresa[11] was never married and yet if ever there was a mother who was a light to those she cared for, she was one! The issue is how can women be a light not only in their children's world but in their families, their communities and in the world? The Biblical answer will be to imbibe the virtues of the woman described in Proverbs 31.

However, while many of us must have read this passage several times and must have listened to several sermons on the virtuous woman, we struggle when it comes to its practical application in our day-to-day lives. How can we become the Proverbs 31 Woman? Here, we discuss some of the virtues that are relevant to motherhood:

"Her children arise and call her blessed."

[Proverbs 31:28a]

Whenever I read this verse, the question that comes to my mind is, why "her children?" After all, the earlier verses described her role as a wife and a home maker. It has now dawned on me that a mother who wants her children to call her 'blessed' must be a Proverbs 31 Woman.

Who then is a Proverbs 31 Woman?

The Proverb 31 Woman earns the

confidence of her husband.

[Proverb 31:11]

If you want your children to "arise and call you blessed", you have to earn the confidence of your husband. Your husband is not naturally wired to have confidence in you. He is wired and commanded to love you [Ephesians 5:23]. It is possible for a husband to love his wife yet not have confidence in her. The confidence has to be earned!

"she considers a field and buys it; out of her earnings she plants a vineyard."

[Proverbs 31:16]

This demonstrates financial prudence – yet another way you can earn your husband's confidence. There is the need to differentiate between economising resources during the time of relative scarcity and wasting or hoarding resources in times of abundance. It is quite possible not to allocate resources efficiently during either time. A prudent manager is one who efficiently allocates available resources during both the times of relative scarcity and relative abundance. This is what a Proverbs 31 wife must do if she must earn her husband's confidence.

Also, to earn your husband's confidence, you need to understand a basic difference between a man and a woman. For example, the woman naturally cares about what she wears and how she looks. Therefore she may like to spend money on clothes, jewellery and other feminine items. However, most men are not very much interested in these. They are more likely to spend money on books, cars, CDs/DVD recorders and players.

These basic gender differences do not necessarily make the woman more wasteful than the man. Financial prudence or lack of it is the point. Ask yourself, what is the opportunity cost[12] of your jewellery? If you have to forgo, delay or postpone the payment of a child's school fees or the rent for your accommodation in order to buy the latest jewellery, clothes or cosmetics, the real cost is not only the money value but also the cost of the other things you have to forego. It is when you consistently make the right/selfless choices with or without your husband that you are likely to win the confidence of your husband.

*"she brings her husband good, **not harm**, all the days of her life."*

[Proverbs 31:12 emphasis added]

Many Christian women may think that verse 12 sounds superfluous since few women (either Christian or non-Christian) will set out to 'do harm' to their husbands. However many women do a lot of 'harm' to their husbands with their minds and mouths, especially if they are married to unbelieving husbands.

They do not think or see anything good in their husbands. Instead of engaging in prayer for the salvation or sanctification of their unbelieving husbands, they engage in 'gossip' about him. Soon everybody knows the details of the unfaithfulness of their husbands becuase of their own indiscretions.

I heard a story of an 'Ijesha'[13] woman who never called her husband by his real name but Oloriburuku which means the 'unfortunate one'. She never spoke anything good about her husband even in the presence of her children. She would refer to her husband when speaking to her children as your unfortunate father - Oloriburuku Baba re. She did not know that her three-year-old child had been taking this in. So when the child was in kindergarten, he was asked for his father's name. He confidently answered Oloriburuku, (the unfortunate one)! Would you blame him? He knew no other name!

Yet I know another child who, when asked for the name of his father answered 'Darling'; yet another said 'Daddy', another 'Dee' and another 'Sweetheart'. Do good to your husband all the days of your life; speak well of him in his presence and in his absence; wish him good; pray good things into his life; do not compete with him, complement him. Even when he does not deserve it, do good to him; even if he seems to be 'controlled' by his mother, still do good to him and support him always. It is then that your children will call you "blessed".

The Proverbs 31 Woman is not lazy but hardworking.

[Proverbs 31:13-19]

The Proverbs 31 Woman is generous especially to the poor and the needy.

[Proverbs 31:20]

The Proverbs 31 Woman watches over the affairs of her household [

Proverbs 31:21-25]

The Proverbs 31 Woman speaks with wisdom and faithful instruction is on her tongue

[Proverbs 31:26]

The Proverb 31 Woman "fears" the Lord

[Proverbs 31:30]

Blessed are you, not only by your children but by God, if you do all these.

Practical Guidelines

According to Kate Douglas Wiggin[14] (1856-1923) your children will only have one mother in the whole world. How then can you ensure that you perform your god-given role of mother to the best of your ability? Here are some answers:

- Let your dignity consist in being unknown to the world; your glory in the esteem of your husband and your pleasures in the happiness of your family.[15]

- Like Rose Elizabeth Kennedy[16] (1890-1995), do not look on motherhood as a work of love and duty alone but also as an honourable profession that demands the best you can bring to it.

- Always remember that children are the sum of what mothers contribute to their lives. So contribute your best spiritually and physically to the lives of your children.[17]

- Always encourage your children to believe that they can be the best in anything. Cultivate a spirit of excellence in them.[18]

- Be your children's bridge between God and their world and when they need to get across, 'steady yourself long enough (for them) to run across safely'.

- Let your love for your children endure through thick and thin.[19]

- Let your knee be 'the best academy' for your children not only in a physical sense but also in the spiritual sense; pray for them always.[20]

Finally, always remember that *"being a full-time mother is one of the highest salaried jobs in my field, since the payment is 'pure love'"*[21] from your children and their father! My daughter's testimony in the Postscript below demonstrates this.

Postscript

My Daughter's Testimony

My mother asked me to share some of my personal thoughts on this beautiful book she has written – *Mothers: The Light of their Children's World* and I am honoured. Unlike my mother, I was raised in a nuclear Christian home, with both my mother and father present throughout my childhood into my adult years. This is a blessing that has formed and shaped the person I am today. How blessed I am indeed to have been brought up by such wonderful and loving parents! How blessed I am to have had such a wonderful role model in my mother!

In this I read about how she describes her mother and the role that she played in her life, though uneducated and with limited resources. There are few similarities between my mother's childhood days and mine, yet there are so many parallels in the role my grandmother played in my mother's life and the role that my mother has, and continues to play in my life. Like her mother, my mother has played an important role in decisions relating to my education, my career, my walk with the Lord and my marriage. I would not be the woman I am today without my mother.

I am fortunate to have a close relationship with my mother as her first daughter, more so now that I am a wife and mother myself. I can say without a doubt that my mother has been a bright light in my life. My mother has always been my 'Number 1' fan; she has been cheering me on in the front row all through my life. She and my father were instrumental in my decision to study law, my chosen career path, and I look back today without any regrets.

My mother has always believed in me and encouraged me to be the best I can be, and in her eyes, I will always be the best. That fact that I am a confident woman today with a healthy self -esteem has a great deal to do with my mother.

On many occasions my mother has told me how beautiful I am, and I might finally be coming round to believing it's true.

One particular incident stands out in my memory. I was in my first year of college, a time when women tend to be consumed with looks and have complexes about their figures; I was not exempt. At that time I was very skinny and somebody had just made a comment about my skinny figure that left me in tears and terrified that there was something wrong with me.

Then, my mother was a lecturer in the University and I ran to her office with tears running down my face. On reaching to her office, I told her what had happened and expressed my fear that there was something wrong with me because I was so skinny and I needed to see a doctor. My mother took me in her arms, held my face in her hands and told me *"Tomi you are beautiful and there is absolutely nothing wrong with you, you are just beautiful the way you are."* Now, more than fifteen years later, my mother continues to tell me how beautiful she thinks I am. I have never told her how much those words mean to me now and how much they meant to me fifteen years ago. I love you mum, you truly make me feel like the most beautiful person in the world, and in your eyes, I am sure I am.

I hope that mothers and mothers-to-be across the world will get to read this book and gain some insight into what it means to be a mother – a light in their children's world.

My mother has been a light in my world – a bright light indeed. She prepared me to be the mother and wife that I am today by loving my father so well, by giving sacrificially to all of us and being the best mother she could be.

Thank you mother, I love you.

Olutomi Ojo-Ade (nee Odejide)

Endnotes

1. Abraham Lincoln (1809-1865).

2. Keith Brooks, http://www.all-famous-quotes.com/Keith_L_Brooks-quotes,html (accessed May 5, 2011).

3. The Modern School system was created for poorer and less brilliant pupils who could not gain admission to standard secondary schools in the Western Region of Nigeria in the 1950s. It was scrapped about a decade after its creation.

4. My maternal aunty, Mrs. Phoebian Fehintola Olagbaiye was a school teacher and was one of the first women to have a western formal education in Ikere-Ekiti, my mother's home town.

5. Renita Weems, http://www.quotesgarden.com/mothers.htm (accessed May 5, 2011). She wrote "I cannot forget my mother. She is my bridge. When I needed to get across, she steadied herself long enough for me to run across safely."

6. Ellen Bailey, http://www.ellenbailey.com/poems/ellen 087.htm (accessed May 7, 2010).

7. Mark Twain (1835-1910).

8. Mike Ayo-Obiremi, Folake Lives On. Nigeria: Printwise Ventures Nig. Ltd., 1997.

9. Chalice Hymnal No. 599; Songs for Lifr. No.22; The Worshiping Church No.535.

10. Paul Newman & Joanne Woodward's – Wedding Vows (January 29, 1958), http:// www. myweddingvows.com/..wedding../paul-newman-and-joanne-woodward (accessed May 5, 2011).

11. Mother Theresa (1910-1997). Mother Theresa, born as Agnes Gonxha Bojaxhiu was a Catholic nun of Albanian ethnicity and Indian citizenship. She won the Nobel Peace Prize in 1979 for her globally recognised and acclaimed work among the poorest of the poor in the slums of Calcutta.

12. Opportunity cost is the cost of the alternative good or need forgone in order to satisfy a particular want.

13. 'Ijesa' is one of the ethnic groups within the Yoruba tribe in Southwestern Nigeria.

14. Kate Douglas Wiggin, http://www.quotesgarden. com/mothers.htm (accessed May 10, 2011). She wrote "Most of all the other beautiful things in life come by twos and threes by dozens and hundreds. Plenty of roses, stars, sunsets, rainbows, brothers, and sisters, aunts and cousins, but only one mother in the whole world."

15. Jean Rousseau (1644-1699). He wrote "Her dignity

consists in being unknown to the world; her glory is in the esteem of her husband; her pleasures in the happiness of her family."

16. Rose Elizabeth Kennedy, http://www.mothers.net/ mothersquotes.12htm (accessed May 16, 2011). She wrote "I looked on child-rearing not only as a work of love and duty but as a profession that was fully as interesting and challenging as any honorable profession in the world and one that demanded the best that I could bring it."

17. George Washington (1732-1799). He wrote "My mother was the most beautiful woman I ever saw. All I am I owe to my mother. I attribute all my success in life to the moral' intellectual and physical education I received from her."

18. Pablo Picasso, http://www.thinkexist.com/ quotation/...i...mother.../143238htm (accessed May 16, 2011). He wrote "When I was a child, my mother said to me 'If you become a soldier, you'll be general. If you become a monk you'll end up as the pope.' Instead I became a painter and wound up as Picasso."

19. Washington Irving (1783-1859). He wrote "A mother is the truest friend we have, when trials, heavy and sudden, fall upon us when adversity takes the place of prosperity when friends who

rejoice with us in our sunshine, desert us when troubles thicken around us, still will she cling to us, and endeavor by her kind precepts and counsels to dissipate the clouds of darkness, and cause peace to return to our hearts."

20. Hosea Ballou (1771-1852). He wrote "Education commences at the mother's knee, and every word spoken within hearsay of little children tends toward the formation of character." " James Russell Lowell (1819-1891). He wrote "The best academy [is] a mother's knee."

21. Mildred B. Vermount, http:// www.thinkexist. com (accessed May 15, 2011). She wrote "Being a fulltime mother is one of the highest salaried jobs in my field, since the payment is pure love."

Other Books By The Authors

On the eve of their 40th wedding anniversary Thomas and Agnes Odejide have chosen to answer a question on so many lips -

'What is your secret to a long and happy marriage?'

The result is a seven book series:

I said 'I Do' Marriage is a Commitment

This is the recently third edition of Thomas' and Agnes' first book on marriage. It contains practical experience about their courtship and subsequent marriage on 16th October 1971 and how they have been able to tackle some of the practical issues of marriage like 'the common purse', in-laws and parenting.

A beautiful aspect of this third edition is that three people who played different roles at their wedding ceremony 40 years ago have been invited give their testimonies. Find out who they are and what they shared.

ISBN 9-789-78384-681-7

The Wife Of My Youth

Thomas' takes the opportunity to write a brave, loving and moving memo to Agnes. He has made it an 'open memo' so that we may all eavesdrop and discover their secret.

This is not a one-sided view. Thomas has invited Agnes to respond, and so we are privy to her reply.

ISBN 9-781-90797-105-1

Mothers: the light of their children's world

How many mothers are thought of as the light of their children's World? Do you wonder (like the author) whether your children think of you as a light in their world? As mothers or mothers- to-be, what are the guidelines to follow that make us a light in our children's world? What is the role of fathers or fathers-to-be in making 'the light' (mothers) shine the more. These and other questions of Christian family life are addressed in this book.

Dr. Agnes Odejide in this book has told the beautiful and moving story of how her mother has 'shaped' her life through her faith in God and therefore made her what she is today. By inviting her husband, Thomas, to write on the husband's role in making the mother to shine the more, she has also emphasises the unity of father and mother in the Christian family.

ISBN 9-781-90797-107-5

Forty years After I said 'I Do'

Every marriage has its ups and downs, but how many marriages are able to withstand the storms of four decades and emerge stronger and better than ever? This is the testimony of Thomas and Agnes who have taken time out of their continuing journey of discovery to share some of the lessons and wisdom they have gleaned along the way.

They remain as enthusiastic for marriage as they were when as a young couple they said 'I do' on 16th October 1971. They are motivated by a passionate desire to see marriages healed and strengthened as they encourage couples to look to God for the agape love only He can provide. This is what will equip them to love and be faithful to their other halves over the long haul.

ISBN 9-781-90797-114-3

Hope for every barren couple

Infertility has been an age-old problem since the beginning of time, and various views abound as to how to address it. This book offers a much-needed dose of hope for couples struggling with infertility. It is exceptional in that it offers a range of holistic insights, beginning with a need to rule out or tackle any physiological causes.

Dr Thomas Odejide combines his medical insights with the cultural and social ramifications identified sympathetically by his wife and co-author, Dr. Agnes. They succeed in debunking the traditional perception that it is solely a female problem. They also offer a spiritual overview drawing on the inspirational biblical accounts of infertility reversed, and the encouragement it brings.

ISBN 9-781-90797-116-7

Better (not) to Marry?

Gone are the days when the romantic high of falling in love was automatically followed by courtship and then the longed-for wedding. It has become a popular trend to avoid marriage which is either viewed as an omen or unnecessary.

The authors, Drs Thomas and Agnes Odejide, are clear that marriage is not for everyone, but they are quick to extol its virtues based on their 40 years of marital experience. The question is posed, and the biblical rationale for marriage made clear, but ultimately, readers must decide this vexing question for themselves. One thing is clear, from the testimonies of the several contributors, marriage is as vibrant and relevant today as it ever was!

ISBN 9-781-90797-118-1

Sexual Intimacy in Marriage - our experience

In this book, Drs. Thomas and Agnes Odejide are brave enough to redress the imbalance whereby the world over-emphasises sex but the church sweeps it under the carpet. Although this concise book is not a sex manual, it serves to debunk some of the common misconceptions and myths couples may retain as they embark on marriage and during the course of marriage.

It has been the authors' experience, both personally and from observation, that when such mind-sets are addressed and removed, this paves the way for wonderful sexual encounters with one's spouse. They refocus Christian couples' attention to the originator of sex, God Himself, and highlight His joyous plan for sex in marriage. They also demonstrate where certain aberrations and perversions have undermined God's plan for sex within marriage and how this has in turn impacted families and society at large.

ISBN 9-781-90797-117-4

As they celebrate 40 years of marriage they felt the call of the Holy Spirit to commence a new ministry 'Family Hope Counselling Ministry International'.

Availability of the Books

All books are available direct from Thomas and Agnes by email bosunode@yahoo.co.uk or feyode45@yahoo.com

All except the 'I said I do Marriage is a Commitment' are available from their publisher Jesus Joy Publishing at their website

www.jesusjoypublishing.co.uk

and www.amazon.co.uk